THIS BOOK
BELONGS TO:

I0165836

Written by Aparna Coutinho

Illustrations and design by John Kelly

First edition March 2025
Printed by Amazon KDP Print on demand Amazon KDP: 978-1-0684256-0-8
Published by Aparna Coutinho

www.aparnacoutinho.com

MEET the iTchiwoos

the best friends you didn't know you had!

Aparna Coutinho **John Kelly**

This is the tale of the Itchiwoos,
Who've been very dear to me,
Since I met them as a little girl
At the tender age of three.

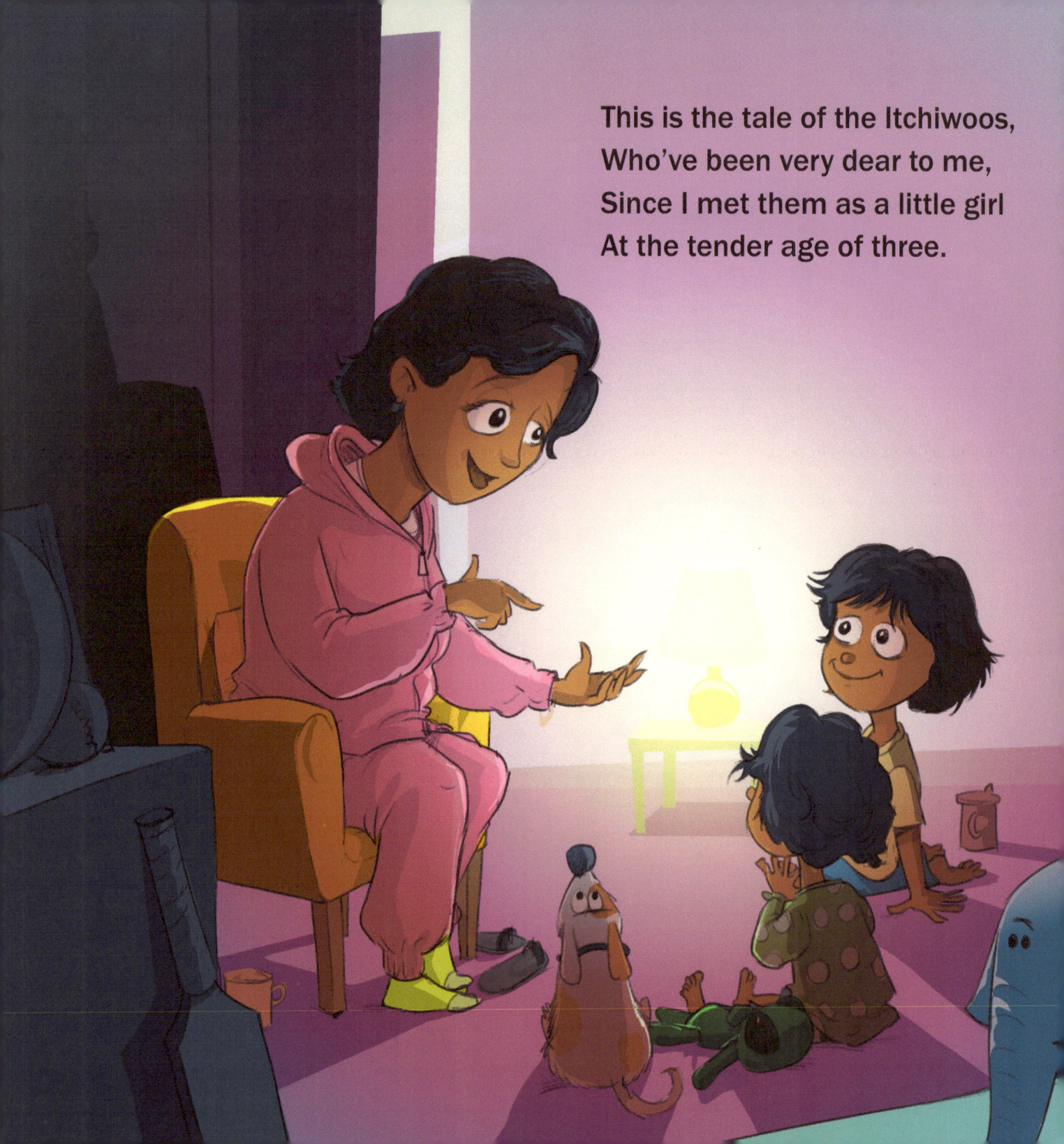

So I want to take a little time
And share the joy they bring
With lovely children just like you,
Let's all join in and sing...

SPACE

Can you **see** the Itchiwoos?

The itchi-kitchi-mitchi-sitchi-titchi-woos.
The gitchi-pitchi-witchi-ritchi-zitchi-woos.

I **see** them...

...can *you?*

The Itchiwoos are a little shy
And prefer to live inside.
So, you'll usually
Only see them...

...from the corner of your eye.

The Itchiwoos are VERY small,

And love to run

and climb

They adore the sun,

But hate the rain,

And the in-betweeny times.

The Itchiwoos
are brightly hued,

Red, yellow, green, and blue.

Their fuzzy tums have stars or spots,
In pink and purple too!

Can you **hear** the Itchiwoos?

The itchi–kitchi–mitchi–sitchi–titchi–woos.
The gitchi–pitchi–witchi–ritchi–zitchi–woos.

I **hear** them...

...can **you?**

The Itchiwoos write
cheeky songs,

BIBBERLY - BOBBERLY!
SQUIGGLY - SPOGGILY!
OOOPA - DEE - DOOPA - DEE
DIDDLY - PING!

With silly
rhyming words.

And *jolly*, happy, *rollicking* tunes...

...that they

tweet

like little birds.

The Itchiwoos have springy tails that BOUNCE them ROUND and ROUND!

Up-down, left-right, and round again,

With a **POINGING! BOINGING!** sound.

What **do** they do, those Itchiwoos?

Those itchi-kitchi-mitchi-sitchi-titchi-woos.
The gitchi-pitchi-witchi-ritchi-zitchi-woos.

I **know** what...

...do you?

Those Itchiwoos are naughty,
Always getting into trouble.

Stealing stinky socks
and pongy pants,
And blowing
toothpaste bubbles.

Pants

SOCKS

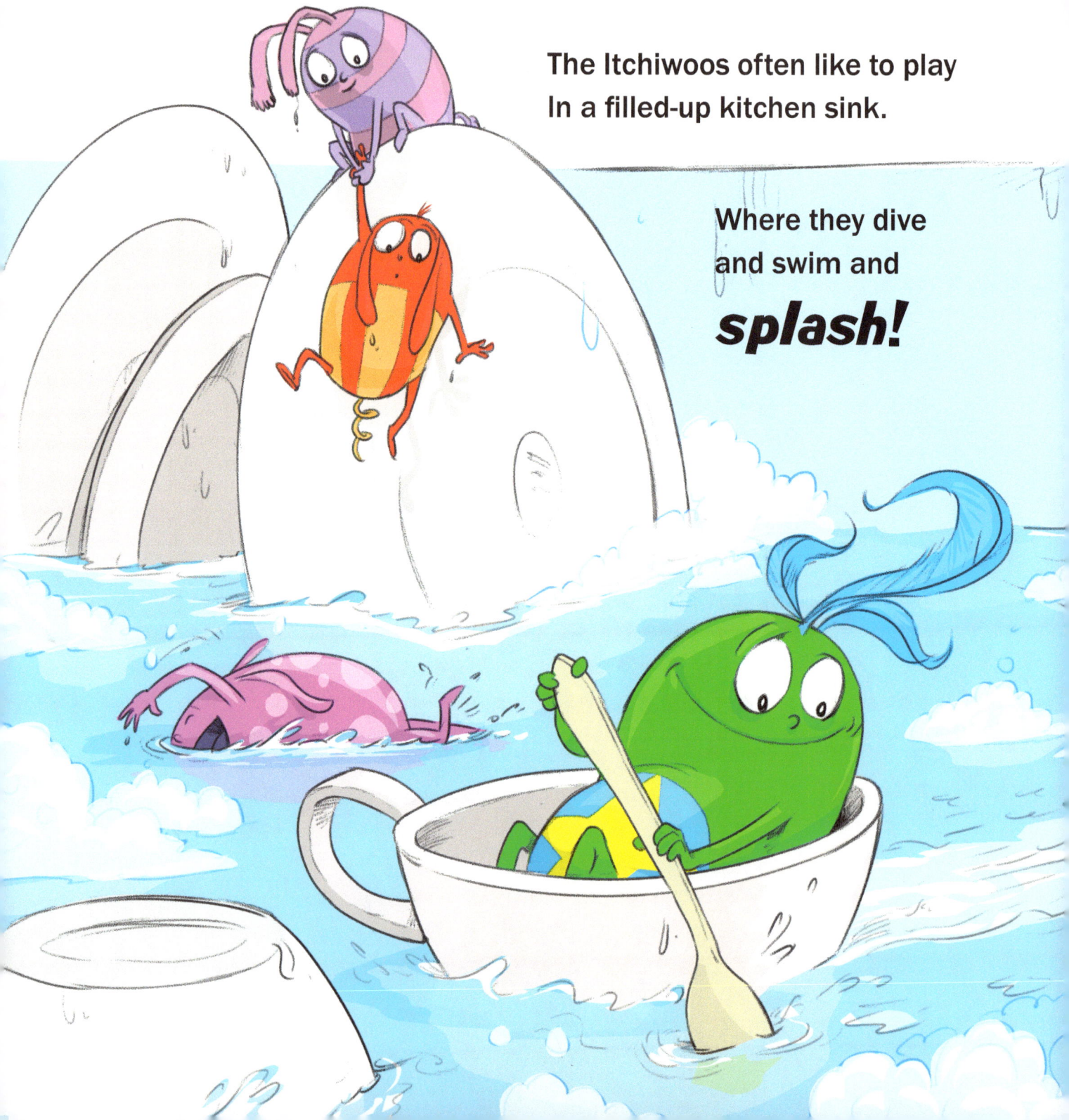

The Itchiwoos often like to play
In a filled-up kitchen sink.

Where they dive
and swim and

splash!

Making the cups
and saucers.
clink.

The Itchiwoos
love noisy foods
that **CRACKLE!**

SNAP!

and

CRUNCH!

They feast on peas and bits of toast,
And fish and chips for lunch.

The Itchiwoos love chocolate,
and foam banana sweets.

They're fond of fresh-baked cinnamon rolls,

And other sticky treats.

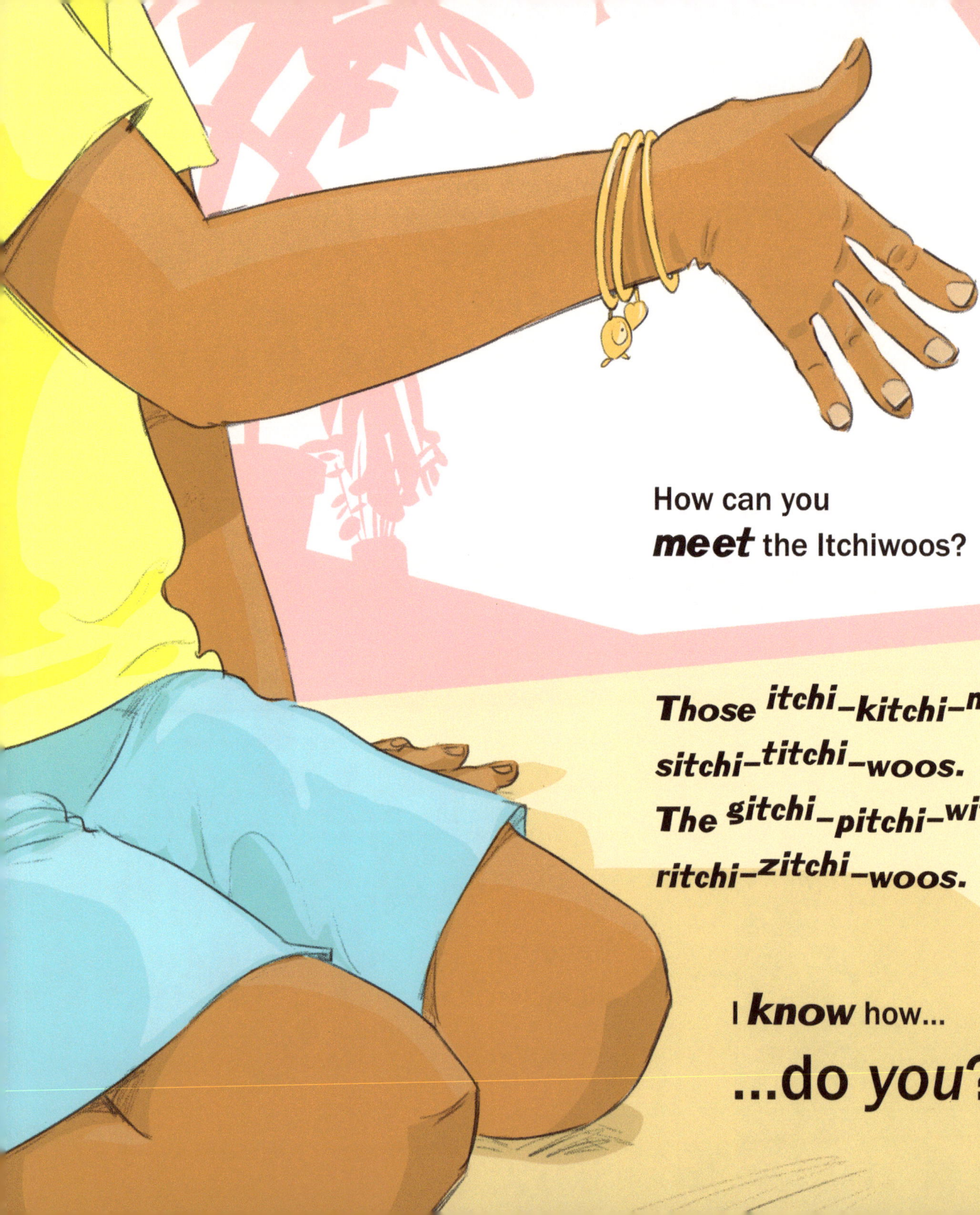

How can you **meet** the Itchiwoos?

Those itchi-kitchi-mitchi-sitchi-titchi-woos.
The gitchi-pitchi-witchi-ritchi-zitchi-woos.

I **know** how...

...**do you?**

The trick is to sit statue-still,
In a spot where they like to play.
And if one spots you,
it will **squeak**...

"*Hi! How are you today?*"

You smile and say,
"I'm very well!"
And add **"Would you
like to play?"**

It happily nods
And smiles and says
**"I'd love to.
Lead the way!"**

You head into the garden
To play catch and hide-and-seek.
Then you twirl around in circles,
Till you trip over your feet.

You lie on the warm grass giggling,
As the sun slowly starts to fade.

Then you say

"let's go up to my room"

"There are more games to be played."

Once in your room,
What do you find,
In a big pile on your bed?
A snuggly family of Itchiwoos
All resting their sleepy heads.

*You're feeling tired
and start to y-a-w-n,
And your Itchiwoo yawns too.*

You both realise the day is done...
...and it's sleepy-time for you.

You climb up on your cosy bed
And burrow in your sheets.
The Itchiwoo cuddles up to you,
And you all fall fast asleep.

Tomorrow brings a brand-new day,
With more adventures to come.
Your new friends, the Itchiwoos, and you
Will wake to **SO** much fun."

Acknowledgements

The author would like to
thank the following.

To my Father for my love of reading, my
Mother for the music, my Sister for the
best squabbles, and most of all to my
darling husband Bradley and two boys
Aylan and Zachary without whom this
book would never have happened.

www.ingramcontent.com/pod-product-compliance
Lightning Source LLC
LaVergne TN
LVHW072120070426
835511LV00002B/43